Walt Grassl's Stand Up & Speak Up

Walt Grassl's Stand Up & Speak Up

Overcome your stage fright
so you can overcome any fear

by Walt Grassl

Published by
RockStar Publishing House
28039 Smyth Drive
Suite 102
Valencia, CA 91355
www.rockstarpublishinghouse.com

Copyright © 2013 by Walt Grassl

All rights reserved. No part of this book may be reproduced or transmitted in any form or by in any means, electronic or mechanical, including photocopying, recording, or by any information storage and retrieval system, without the written permission of the Publisher, except where permitted by law.

Manufactured in the United States of America, or in the United Kingdom when distributed elsewhere.

Grassl, Walt

    Stand Up & Speak Up: Overcome your stage fright so you can overcome any fear

    Worthy Shorts ID: RSP114

    ISBN:

    Paperback: 978-1-937506-36-0

    eBook: 978-1-937506-37-7

    PDF: 978-1-937506-38-4

Cover design by: Dawn Teagarden
Cover photo by: Eno Georgette Inwek
Interior design: Darlene Swanson

www.WaltGrassl.com

Table of Contents

Introduction 1
Stage fright 5
Walt's Rules 9
Just because you couldn't doesn't mean you can't 11
Take small steps 17
When opportunity knocks, answer the door 21
Invest in yourself 25
You can't just study; you have to do the work 29
There is no elevator to success. You have to take the stairs. 31
Use personal stories 35
Perfection is the enemy of progress 39
Make eye contact 41
Record yourself 43
Bo knows: Cross-training is not only for sports 45
Breathe! 49
Set deadlines 51
Be nice to people when you don't need anything from them 53
Stand Up and Speak Up 57

Chapter 1
Introduction

"If you're not going to speak up, how is the world supposed to know you exist?"

– Author unknown

Hello, world!

This is a story of reinvention, a story about how I overcame the number one fear in the world: the fear of public speaking or stage fright.

Just shy of my 50th birthday, the pain of avoiding public speaking finally forced me to take action to address my fear. By sharing my story and the rules I chose to adopt, I hope to inspire you to act on your fear — or, if you are already in the process of fighting your fear, provide some tips that will help make your journey easier.

So you, too, can stand up and speak up, and let the world know you exist.

Walt 1.0

On June 25, 1975, Walt 1.0 was released. I entered the workforce a little more than a month before my 18th birthday.

I was painfully shy when I began my 37-year career with Hughes Aircraft (which later became Raytheon). At the same time, I was going to college.

I graduated from Cal State Long Beach with a BSEE in computer engineering and worked my way up the corporate ladder from technician to engineer to project leader to senior manager.

Walt 1.0 evolved from performer to leader, with minor upgrades along the way. I came to grips with shyness, learned new skills and grew a little bit every day.

Walt 1.0 (June 1975)

But Walt 1.0 had a major flaw: severe stage fright.

Walt 2.0

In August of 2006, at the ripe young age of 49, I began development of Walt 2.0. Finally facing my fear of public speaking, I took the first step by joining Toastmasters.

Toastmasters International is a leader in communication and leadership development. Membership in Toastmasters is one of the most cost-effective skill-building tools available anywhere. In Toastmasters, you will:

- Increase your self-confidence
- Become a better speaker
- Communicate more effectively
- Become a better leader

My initial progress in Toastmasters was slow. In February of 2008, I attended three speaking training events in Las Vegas and realized something on the flight back home: I had a long journey ahead of me, but I *could* conquer stage fright. I set a goal of being good enough to get paid to speak by August of 2012, when I would be 55 and old enough to retire.

Early beta testing of Walt 2.0 included competing in Toastmasters speech contests, doing stand-up comedy on some big stages (the Hollywood Improv and the Flamingo in Las Vegas), and performing in improv and sketch-comedy shows with Held-2gether, in Long Beach, California. Improv, or improvisation, is unscripted comedy. An example of improv is the old TV show *Whose Line Is It Anyway?*. Sketch comedy is scripted short comedy scenes, such as those performed on *Saturday Night Live*.

Walt 2.0 (November 2012)

I retired from Raytheon in August of 2012. And I put the finishing touches on Walt 2.0.

And at the start of 2013, Walt 2.0 was released.

In the first week of the new year, I became the host of an Internet radio show, *Walt Grassl's Stand Up and Speak Up* and began a blog called *Walt 2.0*.

Have fun!

Before I talk about stage fright and how I kicked its behind, I want to remind you to have fun. Enjoy the process of learning.

Most of us can remember learning to ride a bike — not the details, but the initial anxiety, the falling down and getting up, and the joy of eventually getting it right. And the happiness of acquiring a new skill that gave you more freedom and mobility. Remember what it was like to be that 18-year-old? ... What, you were younger when you learned?

Let's talk about stage fright.

Chapter 2
Stage fright

If you have stage fright, you know what it is. At least, you know what it feels like to you. I define stage fright as that perspiring, legs-shaking, hands-shaking, voice-trembling, mind-blanking feeling you get when you speak to a group of people. The larger the group is, the worse the symptoms are.

I have become an expert on stage fright. Not certified by any educational institution but by the school of life. Living with and cowering from that evil beast for the first 50 years of my life. I tried to avoid speaking in public. But many times I couldn't.

I did some research on stage fright, mainly on the Internet. Like the Bible, you can use the Internet to prove either side of any argument. So, caveat emptor. Buyer beware.

- According to the World Health Organization, 75 percent of the world's population suffers from speech anxiety — **three out of four people.**
- According to Speech-topics-help.com, in its Fear of Public Speaking Statistics blog discussing the top 10 global fears, more people would rather die than talk in front of a live audience.

- FreeDictionary.com defines phobia as *an intense but unrealistic fear that can interfere with the ability to socialize, work or go about everyday life, brought on by an object, event or situation.* It goes on to say phobias are among the most treatable mental health problems.

Wait a minute. Does this mean that people who suffer from stage fright are crazy?

In a blog post entitled "Overcoming Stage Fright," M. Farouk Radwan states that stage fright is not caused by any single factor; rather, many factors are responsible for the anxiety we feel when we face an audience.

Having lived with stage fright for more than 50 years, I can tell you how these possible causes that he cited for stage fright applied to me:

- Having a self-image problem – *yes*
- Perfectionism – *definitely*
- Self-consciousness – *yes*
- Fear of embarrassment – *definitely*
- Being afraid that people notice that you are afraid – *a little*
- Fear of being judged in a bad way – *yes*
- Improper breathing – *you're supposed to breathe?*
- Can't remember what you are going to say – *most definitely*

Radwan believes that stage fright is not the cause but the *symptom* of other underlying problems. Find the real reasons and deal with them. Only then will your stage fright disappear.

So what can we say about stage fright?

- Most people suffer from stage fright.

- This means that if you have stage fright, you are normal.

- However, stage fright is a mental illness.

- And it is caused by several underlying factors, which means you don't have just one mental illness but several.

- The good news is, it's curable.

Takeaway

The world is full of people who have overcome or come to grips with their fear of speaking in public.

I overcame stage fright, and so can you.

Chapter 3
Walt's Rules

Steven Covey, who wrote "The 7 Habits of Highly Effective People," said, "I didn't invent the seven habits … I just organized them."

The following chapters in this book contain *Walt's Rules*. But let me be perfectly clear: **I did not invent Walt's Rules;** I just collected them.

The rules are words of wisdom that make it easy to understand the choices I made on my journey to overcome stage fright. These rules apply to overcoming the fear of public speaking as well as making other changes.

Chapter 4
Just because you couldn't doesn't mean you can't

Henry Ford said, "Whether you think you can, or you can't, you're right." I like to say that just because you couldn't do something before doesn't mean you can't do it now. It's a new day. At least I say that now. This change in attitude is fairly new, as you will see.

I can't draw

When I was in first grade, I had a horrific experience with a cat. I sat at our mahogany dining room table, doing my homework. I could hear my mom washing dishes and I could smell the aroma of our spaghetti dinner. And slowly, my paper began getting wet, one drop at a time, from my tears of frustration.

That night's homework assignment involved drawing. A piece of paper was divided into three sections. Each section had a word. My mission, which I had no choice but to accept, was to draw a picture that went with the word.

- Ball, no problem.
- Tree, no problem.
- Cat, **big problem.**

For whatever reason, I could not put lines on paper that in any way resembled a cat.

My dear parents tried to help. They were a couple of patient saints.

After I drew and erased several hideous attempts, my paper was looking like one of the Dead Sea Scrolls. So they had me drawing on pieces of scrap paper — *many* pieces of scrap paper.

Over.
And over.
And over.

Finally, many hours and many tears later, I cried, "I CAN'T DO THIS!"

The next morning, I took the tattered assignment with me to class, along with a pristine note from my parents. The note explained to Mr. Garcia, my first-grade teacher, how I really, really tried to complete the assignment. At least that's what they told me it said.

That night, I labeled myself: "I **can't** draw.

As I grew older, I did what any normal person does. I collected more "can't" labels.

What labels have you collected?

I am not mechanically inclined

In 8th grade, I decided I wanted to attend a technical high school, Don Bosco Technical Institute. I was required to take an entrance exam that had, in addition to English and math sections, a mechanical aptitude section.

A few weeks after taking the exam, I met with the school counselor to review the test results. The first question he asked was, "What major did you choose?"

I hesitatingly replied, "Electronics."

"Good, because if you had said mechanical technology, we would have to talk!"

I acquired another label: "I have no mechanical aptitude."

Reinforcing this label, about six years after graduating from Bosco, I bought a condo and tried to hang a screen door. The first time, I hung it on the wrong part of the doorjamb. The second time, I had the right part of the doorjamb, but the door opened in the wrong direction. Finally, the third time was the charm.

Go ahead and laugh. I do. At the time, my mechanical aptitude WAS lacking.

Over time, my list of **can'ts** continued to grow.

Maybe I can

In the early '90s, my younger brother, Karl, was visiting from Texas.

One day during his visit, I called him to cancel our lunch date because I had to call a plumber to fix my dripping shower. He asked, "Why don't you fix it yourself?"

"I can't. I'm not mechanically inclined."

"I'll come over and we'll figure it out."

While we were figuring it out, he said, "Try to fix everything yourself first. You can always call a repairman later if you mess it up. In the long run, you'll save a lot of money. Besides, just because you couldn't do something before doesn't mean you can't do it now."

That day, we fixed the shower. And we fixed my thinking. That's right: My kid brother changed my thinking.

Just because you couldn't doesn't mean you can't.

A few years later, I was channel-surfing. I came across a drawing show called *Imagination Station*, hosted by Mark Kistler. He used easy-to-follow cartoonish drawings to teach basic drawing skills. I recorded the shows and drew along with him. And now I can draw.

I'm no Leonardo da Vinci, but I can draw. You see, just because you couldn't before doesn't mean you can't now.

In the early 2000s, I mentored Whitney High School's robotics team, leading them in the successful design, from scratch, of robots for the FIRST (For Inspiration and Recognition of Science and Technology) robotics competitions.

I can do mechanical design.

I can't speak in public

I tagged myself with the stage-fright label when I was in elementary school.

Although I was an A student, when I had to go up to the chalkboard in front of the class, the nervousness and paralysis that I felt made me seem... not so bright.

In the early 1990s, Greg Chester, a colleague at Raytheon, told me about Toastmasters. I made excuses and talked myself out of it.

Several traumatic speaking incidents happened in 2006, and I remembered Greg's suggestion and finally decided to join Toastmasters.

In 2008 I attended speaking seminars, took improv and stand-up-comedy classes. I have since spoken to audiences of 300 people, performed stand-up at the Hollywood Improv and the Flamingo in Las Vegas. In 2012, I performed in improv shows and a sketch comedy show.

Just because you couldn't doesn't mean you can't.

Takeaway

I encourage fellow Toastmasters to try improv or stand-up. I often hear:

- I can't.

- I am not funny.

- I could never do that.

Is that how you think? What "I can't" labels do you have?

Remember, **just because you couldn't do something before doesn't mean you can't do it now!**

Chapter 5
Take small steps

In Dr. Robert Maurer's book *One Small Step Can Change Your Life,* he explains how to effectively change behavior. In the book, he shares:

> "For most people, big changes trigger a primal fear, and that fear disables the thinking part of our brain. Then, the thought process that drives change never engages. And change doesn't happen. But, when we take small, comfortable steps, we reduce the fear and melt away the resistance to change. The thinking process engages. And change begins."

Let me share two stories that show how this rule helped me, one about weight loss and the other about stage fright.

Small steps toward weight loss

In May of 2012, I was attending a mastermind meeting–where the "Stand Up and Speak Up" brand was conceived.

What is a mastermind? Napoleon Hill, author of one of the seminal books on personal empowerment, *Think and Grow Rich,* defined the concept of a mastermind as a "coordination of knowledge and effort, in a spirit of harmony, between two or more people, for the attainment of a

In the vicinity of 280 pounds

definite purpose." In other words, a group of people who join forces to accomplish a specific goal.

I also had a more powerful life change come out of the meeting.

One of the mastermind group members, Bobby Kelly, a fitness expert from Phoenix, talked about his book on fitness and gave each of us a copy. I read mine that night and I decided to make time to talk to Bobby during a break the next day (because that's what you do at a mastermind).

I talked about how I wanted to start getting fit in a few months, when I retired. I was going to start walking. After describing the toll my almost 55 years on the planet had taken on my body, he calmly looked me in the eye and asked, "Why can't you start walking now, on the days you don't go to work?"

I couldn't tell him the lies I told myself. I admitted that there was no real reason.

I returned home from the mastermind the day before the four-day Memorial Day Weekend and I walked each day.

On Tuesday, as I drove home from my first day back at work, I was thinking I wouldn't walk that night. But when I got home, it was still light, and I chose to walk again. And I kept it up. I walked every day, with very few exceptions. I posted my walking activity on Facebook, and friends (including friends from the mastermind) encouraged me via LIKEs and comments. And I heeded Bobby's dietary advice… a little bit. And I was losing a pound a week.

At the end of November, I made more-radical dietary changes — permanent lifestyle changes, not a diet — and I began working with a personal trainer. I started losing a pound every two days. I was excited to return to the mastermind, less of a man.

In January of 2013, the mastermind group met again. I received so much positive recognition from my mastermind partners after losing 45 pounds, and I had a great reunion with Bobby. I thanked him for asking me the question that led me to decide to take action to change my behavior.

As I write this, I am still losing weight.

After losing 45 pounds in six and a half months

Small steps toward overcoming stage fright

I did not conquer stage fright overnight. It took a series of steps, summarized here:

- Realized I had to change
- Joined Toastmasters
- Attended Toastmasters Area, Division and District Conferences
- Spoke only 6 times in 18 months
- Attended Speaking Training
- Enrolled in improv classes

- Enrolled in standup classes
- Performed standup
- Competed in every Toastmasters speech contest

At each step along the way, I felt better about speaking. The more steps I took, the less I was afraid.

Take away

Chinese philosopher Lao-tzu said, "A *journey of a thousand miles begins with a single step.*" It's like Dr. Maurer's advice, that when we take small, comfortable steps, we reduce the fear and melt away the resistance to change.

If you want to overcome your fear of public speaking or change any behavior, you have to take that first small step.

Chapter 6
When opportunity knocks, answer the door

My first opportunity to join Toastmasters knocked in 1990, when a well-meaning colleague named Greg Chester told me about Toastmasters and how it would help me grow as a speaker and a leader. But I was so afraid of speaking in public that I didn't answer the door.

Fortunately, in August of 2006, another opportunity to join Toastmasters knocked, and this time I opened the door. When I did, it exposed me to other doors of opportunity. Each time I opened another door, I had a wonderful experience and access to even more doors.

Taking those opportunities has given me an exciting five-year journey. If *you* don't answer the door when opportunity knocks, you may be depriving yourself of your own exciting journey.

Please, if you are not already a member of Toastmasters, consider joining. If you are a Toastmaster, are you getting the most out of the opportunities that come with being a Toastmaster?

Your first opportunity is giving and watching speeches in your club. I learn something new every week. The second opportunity is watching speeches outside your club by attending area, division and district speech contests, watching better speakers compete.

I had additional opportunities through Toastmasters to attend special educational meetings. When opportunity knocked to become a club officer, I answered and then was "required" to attend officer training twice a year. At the training, there were breakout sessions on the art of speaking.

I had the opportunity to run for the board of the Raytheon Management Club (I was asked to run and said yes). I was assigned to speaker programs, and I arranged to have "the voice of Raytheon," Pat Coulter, be one of the speakers. I selfishly wanted to pump him for speaking secrets. I asked him to share stories of Raytheon AND how to be an effective speaker. Turns out that although he makes it look effortless, he puts hours and hours of preparation into each of his speaking engagements.

I seized the opportunity to do the introduction, introducing him to a crowd of 200 people and putting my new, improving skills to work. I managed to conceal my nerves and made it through, but I was so nervous that it's just a blur in my memory.

When opportunity knocks, open that door!

In 2007, I went to the fall district Toastmasters conference, where Darren LaCroix, a stand-up comedian and World Champion of Public Speaking, was giving the keynote. I decided to buy some of his training materials, **even before he spoke**. While completing the transaction, he told me about his Champions EDGE network (EDGENet) and made me an offer I couldn't refuse: If I signed up for EDGENet, I would get a discount on my purchase larger than the first month's dues. If I wasn't happy, I could cancel. There was nothing to lose, so I joined.

I began receiving weekly 10-minute audio lessons and a monthly hour-long conference call. I learned various aspects of being an effective speaker and began incorporating them in my speaking.

When opportunity knocks, open that door!

EDGENet provided some training opportunities. Early in February of 2008, I attended a two-day storytelling camp in Las Vegas with Darren LaCroix and Craig Valentine, another World Champion of Public Speaking. They taught us how to make a point by telling a story and how to make your story entertaining.

Later in February, I went to Vegas for five days of training. First was a two-day humor camp, with Darren and Vegas comedian Vinnie Favorito, followed by a day with EDGENet members. Then, there was a two-day seminar with Craig, Darren, Ed Tate (another World Champion of Public Speaking) and Patricia Fripp (a member of the National Speakers Association Hall of Fame). On the plane ride back from those five days of training and networking with professional speakers, I set a goal of becoming a *paid* motivational speaker by August of 2012, when I would turn 55.

Opportunity knocked to attend a stand-up comedy class and I said yes. It resulted in a performance at the Hollywood Improv in March of 2009.

Opportunity knocked to get one-on-one coaching with a Vegas comedian and I said yes. I twice did a five-minute routine on a Saturday night at the Flamingo in Las Vegas.

Opportunity knocked to take improv classes and I said yes. It resulted in being able to perform in two improv shows in 2012.

Opportunity knocked to take a sketch-comedy class and I said yes. I performed in a sketch-comedy show in November 2012.

Opportunity knocked to host a radio show on the RockStar Radio Network and I said yes. In January 2013, I started hosting *Walt Grassl's Stand Up & Speak Up*.

None of this would have been possible if I hadn't answered when the second opportunity to join Toastmasters came knocking. What opportunities are you missing?

Takeaway

Answer when opportunity comes knocking, and follow these rules for expanding your opportunities:

- Never turn down stage time
- Say *Yes*, and figure it out later
- Just show up

Opportunities to speak come up in many ways. You may be directly asked to speak. Never turn it down. My stand-up-comedy mentor told me, "If you ever say no when I offer you a chance to perform, we are done working together!" After several months of working with him, when I showed up in Las Vegas for our two-day coaching session, he said, "I am going to put you on my show tomorrow night! Are you OK with that?" Of course I said yes. Was I nervous? Yes. Did I do it anyway? Yes. Did I live to tell about it? Heck, yes!

Opportunities also come indirectly. You may see a flyer for speech training, a stand-up workshop or an improv class. When an opportunity to speak comes up, say "yes" and then figure out how you will get prepared in time.

And when you sign up for these events, don't get cold feet. Don't leave your future growth at the altar. Show up. Get the experience. Grow. Each time you do it, it will get easier and easier and you will build momentum. You will feel so great about what you accomplish, you might even write a book about it.

Chapter 7
Invest in yourself

Have you ever denied yourself the opportunity to get better at a hobby or skill because you couldn't justify spending money on yourself?

That used to be me. Always wanting to get better but trying to do so on the cheap. I would not pay out of my own pocket for personal coaching or training.

Sometimes I was successful. I taught myself how to bowl by reading books. Went from barely breaking 100 to having a 200 average. I even rolled a 286.

But other times, I was not so successful.

10,000 hours to become an expert

Dr. David Levitin, author of the book *This Is Your Brain on Music*, observed that 10,000 hours of practice is required to become a world-class expert musician. David Seah, computer-game programmer and blogger breaks it down like this:

- at 1 hour … you know some basics
- at 10 hours … you have a pretty good grasp of the basics
- at 100 hours … you are fairly expert

- at 1,000 hours … you are an experienced expert
- at 10,000 hours … you are a master

This formula worked for me. Sometimes. Take bowling, for example.

What if you invested 10,000 hours to master a skill but all that time you were using poor technique?

It was a Sunday morning. May 20, 2006. I was at the Lakewood Country Club for the monthly men's club tournament. I was playing with my regular foursome, which included David Miller, who's about my height and build. The ground was covered with dew, there was still a little ground fog, and the sun was just coming up. It was a beautiful day for golf.

As the day warmed up, my game didn't. My game had plateaued … and not at a level I was happy with. David was playing much better than he had in the past … for the entire round. While waiting to tee off on the 18th hole, I went over to David.

> "So, David, what gives? You're hitting the ball long and straight. What did you do, buy a new set of clubs?"
>
> "Nah, Walt. My son is in the Junior Golf program at Heartwell. His instructor is really, really good. So I took some private lessons … and they are truly paying off. I feel a whole lot better about my game. Did I mention he is really, really good?"
>
> "He must be. You're doing very well. Keep it up."

Hmmmm … Maybe I should take some private lessons. I thought. Nahhhhhh, that's too expensive.

I learned to play golf in 2003. I took a set of "inexpensive" group lessons through the city of Lakewood's parks and recreation department. I read books and magazines. I went to the driving range to try to put into practice what I had read. Any thought of private lessons was quickly eliminated from my mind.

I improved slightly, going from terrible to bad. But … I would hit a good shot just often enough to tell myself, "If I could just do that all the time… All I need is more practice."

A month later, we played again. David was playing well again … and I was not. My frustration grew.

Since I walk the course vs. riding a cart, it gives me time to think in-between shots. If you had been inside my head (and there is a lot of room there), you would have seen the wheels spinning. I thought about my boss Ric Pozo, a great leader, and his attitude about training. When the division had a training goal of 20 hours per person, Ric set a goal for his center of 30 hours per person. When engineering upped its goal to 30, he went to 40. He challenged his leadership team to keep people off of overhead and control other overhead costs, to have more money for training. Ric taught us that training is an important investment in our people.

Have you ever been told by your management, when overhead budgets are cut, that they are freezing the training budget (that is, treating training as an expense)?

How do **you** see training? As an expense or an investment?

I decided to make getting better at golf an investment in myself.

I kept this revelation to myself until the 18th hole. At the tee box, I approached David.

> "David, what's the name of your coach? Can I get his number?"
>
> "Danny Lee. Sure, send me an email and I'll get it to you. And tell him I want a referral fee."

I contacted Danny and arranged to take six weekly lessons. And then six more, for a total of 12 weeks of lessons!

I paid for lessons!

And I practiced what I learned. My handicap went down by 10 strokes. While I could improve in bowling by reading books and watching video, it took coaching and training to improve at golf.

My golf lessons wrapped up in August 2006, around the same time I joined Toastmasters.

Takeaway

As you saw in the previous chapter, I had lots of opportunities to invest in myself. As a result of these investments, I've overcome my fear of public speaking. I have become a speaker, stand-up comedian, improv performer, emcee and radio show host. I am enjoying life like never before. All this happened because I decided that spending money to improve myself was an investment, not an expense.

Don't try to cheap your way to greatness. Invest in yourself.

Chapter 8
You can't just study; you have to do the work

Larry Broughton, an extremely successful entrepreneur and one of the mentors in my mastermind group, posted this on Facebook on Jan 29, 2013:

> "Don't get sucked into the 'Knowledge is power' myth. Way too often, I see seminar and education junkies who get frustrated that they're 'investing' so much in their education and personal/professional development, but not realizing change in their lives or business. Knowledge is only part of the equation… Possessing knowledge without taking action is just useless trivia!"

I relate strongly to that. For the first several years of my journey to overcome stage fright, I bought training CDs and DVDs and attended seminars. I became increasingly knowledgeable about speaking. But I didn't speak. I could write a great speech, but I was too afraid to deliver it.

I knew then that I had to live the mantra "Never turn down stage time." I had to not only say yes if asked to speak but also seek out opportunities to speak.

What did this mean?

Toastmasters has two speech contests in the spring and two speech contests in the fall. I made a decision to compete in all of them.

The point wasn't to win the contest; it was to speak more often. And when you compete in a contest, you prepare more than you do for a speech at a club meeting. And it worked. The more I spoke, the easier it became.

It also meant being prepared to speak for five to seven minutes at a club meeting if no one else had a prepared speech. Were those speeches great? No. But I was learning to speak from my heart and be in the moment.

In the next chapter, we will expand on this concept.

Takeaway

You cannot study your way to overcoming your fear of public speaking. First, learn. Then, speak — often!

Chapter 9
There is no elevator to success. You have to take the stairs.

Let's say you wanted to be the next Tiger Woods. Would you buy a set of golf clubs, read a few golf books and enter a golf tournament?

If you wanted to be a bodybuilder, would you buy some weights, buy the latest issue of *Muscle & Fitness* and enter a bodybuilding competition next week?

We live in a world of instant gratification. Why do you think Staples came up with the EASY BUTTON?

When someone wants to lose weight, what's the first thing they look for? The easy way, of course. A pill. Liposuction.

But there is no elevator to success. You have to take the stairs.

If you want to be successful in anything, you have to follow three simple steps:

- Learn
- Practice
- Perform

You can't just dive into something and be successful, even if you have natural-born talent.

I have a confession to make. I tried to take the elevator to qualify for my local Toastmasters Speakers Bureau. But I failed because I didn't follow this process.

If I had passed my qualifying speech, it would have been a fluke and I wouldn't have had any further success.

I didn't take the stairs and I failed.

You must spend the right amount of time in each of these steps; otherwise, don't expect to be anything better than average. But when you follow this strategy, are dedicated and, most of all, have **patience,** you can master any skill.

The key is **balance**.

If you spend too much time studying but never practice, you will not be able to perform — definitely not under pressure.

In trying to qualify for the speakers bureau, **I didn't put in the practice time,** didn't give enough speeches and didn't do that particular speech often enough. My resulting failure shouldn't have been a surprise.

Learn

Once you realize how important the learning curve for most skills is, you'll start to love the learning phase. Gathering knowledge. Gaining insights.

I love attending classes and getting books and videos on speaking. I used that same approach when I took up bowling, golf and coaching youth basketball. I like to learn a lot before I get out there and try it. It's a good idea to have a clear foundation, a clear understanding, before you try the skill.

Practice

This is the phase most often neglected. This is the phase I neglected on my road to the speakers bureau.

Sometimes we think that, because we read the books and observe the best speakers, once we get on stage we will be able to speak like a pro.

But when we get on stage, reality sets in. Knowledge is great, but skill doesn't come from the knowledge. Knowledge gives us an idea of how to practice the skill.

Skill comes from the practice.

I heard World Champion of Public Speaking Lance Miller say, "Amateurs practice until they get it right. Experts practice until they can't get it wrong."

Perform

To master any skill, you must perform. You must test yourself, and then analyze your performance. Solicit feedback, listen to voice recordings or watch video.

Comedian and actor Steve Martin, in his biography, *Born Standing Up: A Comic's Life*, told how he kept a notebook as a young performer and wrote down how each joke was received by the audience and then he summarized how he could make the show better next time.

When you find something to improve, go back to the learning phase. Make sure you have the knowledge right. Then practice again. And continue to test your skills in real-world situations.

Takeaway

Follow the "Learn, Practice, Perform" cycle and you'll become the master of anything you set your mind to. Don't look for shortcuts. Be patient.

- Spend time learning.

- Spend time practicing.

- Spend time performing.

There is no elevator to success. You have to take the stairs.

Chapter 10
Use personal stories

Bill Gove, the first president of the National Speakers Association, summarized the essence of public speaking in six words: "Tell a story, make a point."

I can remember being given this assignment on more than one occasion in high school English class: Write an essay on any subject you want, in an hour. And I would spend 45 minutes of the hour agonizing over what to write about. I was afraid someone would judge me.

I had a similar experience when I joined Toastmasters. I was afraid to share personal stories. Storytelling expert and World Champion of Public Speaking Craig Valentine taught me the value of telling your stories. Rather than judging you by your story, audiences want to hear your story … because it is new to them.

If you speak about a story you read in the best-selling *Chicken Soup for the Soul* series, or about a book you read, or about an article from the Sunday paper, chances are some people in the audience will have heard it before and may tune you out.

Where do you find stories?
You might not believe it, but stories are all around you.

Martin Presse, who has also studied storytelling with World Champion of Public Speaking Craig Valentine, was a guest on my radio show recently and shared his "Four F's" for finding stories:

- Firsts
- Fears
- Frustrations
- Flaws

I've sprinkled such stories throughout this book to illustrate certain points: the first time I performed stand-up; my fear of public speaking; my frustration with lack of progress and speaking only six times in the first 18 months of Toastmasters; my flaws… Enough said.

Why stories work

When I heard Lisa Cron, the author of *Wired For Story*, speak on storytelling, she pointed out that stories are how we make sense of the world.

Stories transform facts, ideas and abstract concepts into something we can feel. The brain doesn't learn by thinking in the abstract. We are wired not to change. So the analytic brain pokes holes in the changer's facts. But stories create empathy and move people to change. Facts don't change behavior; stories do!

Stories have power because they connect with emotions. Cron describes a story as:

- how what happens (plot) affects someone (protagonist) in pursuit of a difficult quest (problem) and how that person changes as a result
- a protagonist with a driving need that predates the plot; the plot is the pursuit

Advertisers get this! Filmmakers get this! Stories work. Use them in your speeches.

Stories can help you overcome stage fright

If one of your stage-fright symptoms is that your mind goes blank, story-telling helps. Rather than trying to remember facts, data and analysis, you can just relive the story. It happened to you. Just tell it. If you get a detail wrong, it's not important. If the name of your teacher who taught you the life lesson escapes you, just make one up on the spot.

Takeaway

Stories are how we connect with our audience in a memorable way. We all have stories, and they are much easier to remember than facts and data.

Your audience is waiting to hear your story.

Chapter 11
Perfection is the enemy of progress

Perfectionism is one of Radwan's underlying causes of stage fright (see Chapter 2). Our speech is not perfectly written. We know we won't deliver it perfectly. We know we need to practice it more. All true. But with that attitude, we will never get better. Imagine if we all thought that way when we were babies, if we knew we wouldn't walk perfectly the first time we tried, so we didn't keep trying. Imagine what that world would look like.

I was more guilty of this than most. It took me 18 months to give my first six Toastmaster speeches. Many beginning Toastmasters have a similar story, taking somewhere from six months to a year to do six speeches. We don't want to speak unless our speech is perfectly written and perfectly rehearsed.

During my aerospace career, I managed many projects, and I tried to follow a saying that builds off a quote by General George S. Patton:

> "A good plan today is better than a perfect plan tomorrow, because no plan is perfect and tomorrow never comes."

The same is true for speeches. A good speech today is better than a perfect speech tomorrow, because no speech is perfect and tomorrow never comes.

You only get better by speaking. So commit to a date to speak, and speak. You will grow more by giving that speech and learning from it than by polishing it and practicing it more.

Don't try to be like I was; learn from my experience.

Takeaway

A good speech today is better than a perfect speech tomorrow, because no speech is perfect and tomorrow never comes.

Chapter 12
Make eye contact

In February of 2008, while attending several days of training in Las Vegas, I went on a search for my Holy Grail. I was on a quest for the secret to overcoming stage fright — that one trick that I just knew all speakers used.

I asked dozens of total strangers (both audience members and presenters), but I couldn't find that one thing that would cure my stage fright.

However, over the next couple of months, I began making eye contact with members of the audience and started to be much less afraid when speaking. Let me explain why.

Even in my twenties, I was extremely shy. I could not talk one-on-one with a stranger, much less talk to an audience. After years of working on it, I got better.

Then I would be at a party, and a third person would join in the conversation and mess me up. I wasn't comfortable dividing my attention between two people. Over time, I finally got over it.

Then, in my fifties, I heard several speakers coach the importance of eye contact. And how you should scan the room. Other speaking coaches taught the importance of speaking conversationally to your audience.

I began to use both of these concepts. I would make eye contact with a member of the audience near the front and have a conversation with them for a sentence or two. Then, I would find a different member of the audience several seats away, make eye contact, and continue the conversation. And repeat. And I found I was much less nervous. In bigger rooms, as I moved my eye contact to the people in the back of the room, the connection would begin to weaken and I would start to get nervous again. But then I would return to my newfound friends in the front row.

I would get complimented on how well I made eye contact. I didn't mention that it was the only way I could keep from freezing up.

I had found my Holy Grail. I could move past my fear and learn to be a good speaker.

Takeaway

When you first take the stage, before you speak, scan the room. Once you start speaking, have conversations with different people in the audience, one at a time. Say a thought or two to one person, and then move to another, working your way around the room.

Chapter 13
Record yourself

In Steve Martin's book, he tells how, as a teenage comedian, he kept scrupulous records about how each joke was received at every performance (for the Cub Scouts or Kiwanis Club) and then summarized and planned how to make the show better next time.

Several of the mentors I have mentioned in this book give a similar message, updated for the times:

- Record yourself every time you speak
- Video is better than audio

I can hear some of you now: "I hate the way I look and sound when I speak."

World Champion of Public Speaking Darren LaCroix says, "If your audience has to watch and hear you speak, why shouldn't you?"

I hate it too. It often takes days for me to watch or listen, but I do. I even post the speeches on my YouTube channel, waltgrassl.

While people can give you feedback and you may think you understand it, nothing beats seeing and hearing yourself speak.

The 10:1 ratio
World Champion of Public Speaking Craig Valentine says you feel 10 times more nervous than you appear to the audience. Once I learned that, I became less nervous. You can see that for yourself on the video.

How to review a video of a speech

Here's a four-part technique that I think is extremely important to follow. It is recommended by World Champion of Public Speaking Lance Miller:

1. Listen to words without watching the screen. You will learn how your speech sounds.

2. Watch the speech with the sound off. You will see the story your body language tells.

3. Watch it in reverse or fast forward. You will notice repetitive tics or gestures that aren't apparent at regular speed. (For example, if you push your glasses up every 15 seconds, at fast speed you look like you are poking yourself in the head.)

4. Look at the combination and see how it feels.

Like getting over stage fright, the more you watch yourself, the easier it becomes.

Takeaway

Recording yourself is the best feedback you can get. As painful as it is, you need to see and hear yourself just as the audience sees and hears you. I not only record my speeches but also post them on my YouTube channel, waltgrassl.

Chapter 14
Bo knows: Cross-training is not only for sports

Starting in 1989, Nike popularized the cross-training concept with a series of commercials featuring Bo Jackson, at the time an all-star athlete in two professional sports, baseball and football. The ads showed Bo wearing a new type of sneaker, the cross-trainer, and playing different sports, with the message "Bo knows football, Bo knows baseball, Bo knows track," and so on. You can find these commercials on YouTube.

Cross-training began to be discussed in athletics when studies indicated that runners who added biking and swimming to their training regimen performed better than if they trained only by running. But cross-training applies to more than sports.

Cross-training for project leadership

Before I applied the cross-training concept to speaking, I applied it to being a project leader. I often struggled when I was thrown into a group of strangers on a new project and had to immediately take charge. I become a Little League baseball and adult softball umpire to help me improve this skill.

I had played baseball in high school. Then I played softball in work leagues. In 1988, as arthritic knees began to limit my mobility, I could see my softball career winding down. Umpiring would provide an opportunity to stay in the game and provide a service.

As an engineer moving into leadership, it was also an opportunity to go into a situation with a large group of strangers and have to take charge. And it worked.

Cross-training for public speaking

I did not improve my public speaking through Toastmasters alone. I added improv and stand-up-comedy training to complement the speaking skills I'd learned in Toastmasters. How?

Improv

Improv helped me with several aspects of being comfortable as a speaker:

- Trusting that I can pull information from my head
- Being in the moment
- Taking on a point of view
- Taking on emotions
- Physicality

One form of stage fright is the mind going blank. Maybe you know the feeling. I've had it. I used to try to memorize my speech word for word, but when I spoke, it was obvious I was reading the teleprompter in my head. For that reason, my speeches lacked emotion and vocal variety. The fear of my mind going blank was always present. Performing unscripted comedy teaches you to trust that in any situation, you can extract information that exists in your head.

Have you ever been in the situation of listening to a speech and a cell phone rang, or a car alarm went off, or the lights went out? Did the speaker continue along as if nothing had happened? You were probably thinking, is this person talking to us or reciting a speech? Improv teaches you to be in the moment. If it ever happens to you, take the "gift" of the cell phone ringing, briefly acknowledge it so that everyone else can acknowledge it, and then continue your speech. You will have a much stronger connection to the audience than if you ignore it.

Taking on a point of view. Just as improv characters need to have a point of view, so should speakers. Before you speak, consider your point of view and make sure your words, your voice and your body are consistent with it.

Showing emotions. Speaking is not acting. But when you are telling a story and using dialog, that part of your speech can be acting. If a character in the dialog is angry, it's OK to deliver the dialog with anger. Mixing dialog and narration is a key to successful storytelling.

Improv players use space work, the manipulation of imaginary objects to immediately create a scene. In improv, you learn to use your hands and body with a purpose. A speaker should not make random gestures with his hands but rather have a natural purpose for every gesture. Improv helps develop that skill.

Stand-up Comedy

Stand-up comedy helped me in two ways. First, performing as a stand-up in front of 200 people well into their two-drink minimum was at first terrifying but immediately afterward so exhilarating that the fear of speaking decreased measurably. Second, I learned how to connect with an audience through humor. I began to use organic humor in all my speeches.

Emcee, Sketch Comedy

I also had a few opportunities to be an emcee. The stage time in front of an audience helped my comfort level as well.

And recently, I performed in a sketch-comedy show. My original purpose was to learn to write sketches, which would help me write speeches, but then I chose to perform in the sketch show, which helped me learn lines and deliver them naturally.

Takeaway

Whether you want to improve your public speaking skills or any other skills, look for other activities that will benefit you in that quest. I used stand-up and improv to help me conquer stage fright. What will you use to help you overcome your fears?

Chapter 15
Breathe!

The voice is the speaker's instrument. I recently attended a voice workshop to learn to improv my speaking voice. It's not that I was hoping they would teach me to speak in a sexy baritone, like Barry White. OK, it was, but only for a few seconds until I did a reality check.

I learned that you speak with your whole body, from the soles of your feet up. You need to be grounded yet loose. But the biggest thing I learned was that I didn't know how to breathe. More accurately, I'm a shallow breather. No, not the kind that calls you in the middle of the night and hangs up. I take shallow breaths that strain my vocal cords.

The proper way to breathe is to take deep breaths. I realized I have the same issue when I exercise. I sometimes get lightheaded because of improper breathing. The good news is I can practice breathing when I'm working out, and it should help my speaking as well.

Improper breathing is one of Radwan's underlying causes of stage fright (see Chapter 2). This makes even more sense when you consider that deep breathing is an age-old relaxation technique.

Takeaway
Consider voice coaching, or at least learn to breathe properly. It will prevent you from straining your vocal chords, make you a more powerful speaker, and help put you in a relaxed physical state.

Chapter 16
Set deadlines

Napoleon Hill said, "A goal is a dream with a deadline." This rule applies to my journey in a big way. I mentioned earlier that it took me 18 months to give my first six Toastmaster speeches. Why? There was no sense of urgency. I joined Toastmasters to get over my fear of public speaking, period. Whenever.

What changed after 18 months? When I was flying back from Las Vegas in February of 2008, I set the goal of being good enough to get paid to speak by August of 2012, when I would be 55 and old enough to retire.

Even though my deadline was more than three years away, it was specific. I had made miniscule improvements in my battle over stage fright. I knew I needed to speak more often or there was no way I would be ready to get paid to speak. I started speaking more often and taking the other steps mentioned in this book because I had a *deadline* to meet.

Takeaway

When you join Toastmasters, set a goal of how often you want to speak: every two weeks, once a month, every six weeks, whatever you decide. Then hold yourself accountable and meet the deadlines.

Plan to start competing sooner, rather than later, in Toastmasters speech contests. It is not about winning — I repeat. It is *not* about *winning*. The contest has a date, which is a deadline. You're forcing yourself to speak on that date.

Don't be a rudderless ship drifting through your Toastmasters journey. Make your dream of being a confident speaker a reality by setting deadlines.

Chapter 17
Be nice to people when you don't need anything from them

If shyness is a source of your stage fright, here are a couple of tips I practice regularly that will help you get more comfortable with people.

How to enter a room

When I first started to work, I worked in a lab full of older men … who pretty much allowed me to keep to myself. About three years into my career, that changed.

I was assigned to work in a lab with two women who were electronics assemblers, Lil and Priscilla. Lil was a soft-spoken, quiet lady. Priscilla was short and had the most expressive eyes I'd ever seen.

They taught me a lot and played a big part in my career development.

I was very shy, so I would walk into the lab in the morning, and if the ladies were busy working or talking, I'd quietly go to my desk, because I didn't want to disturb them. After a few days of this, Priscilla came over to me and said:

"Young man, did we do something to offend you?"

"No."

"You know, when you enter a room, you should be polite and *speak*."

Lil nodded in agreement.

Wow … My shyness was actually *offending* them. Something had to change! From then on I made it a point to say hi when I arrived each day, regardless of what they were doing. "Good morning, ladies."

When you enter a room, acknowledge the people in the room, verbally or with a nod, whatever is most appropriate.

Be nice to people when you don't need anything from them

Not long after teaching me to "speak," Priscilla taught me another simple leadership lesson: Be nice.

You might be thinking you have run into some leaders who are not nice or some who are downright mean-spirited.

Ask yourself, are these leaders truly effective? Or do they sacrifice long-term effectiveness for short-term results? Do they kill the geese that lay the golden eggs?

One morning, we were all very busy in the lab. An older engineer named Ed walked in, went over to Priscilla and started to engage her in polite conversation, and she replied with one-word answers.

"Hi, Priscilla. How are you?"

"Fine."

"How was your weekend?"

"Fine."

"How is your daughter?"

"Fine."

"Is she still in college?"

"Yes."

This went on for 10 minutes. Then Ed's true agenda came out.

"Priscilla, can you please get this hot job done for me by the end of the day?"

"OK."

Ed left, and Priscilla stood up and marched over to my desk.

"Young man, did you see what just happened?"

"Uh, yes, Priscilla, I think so. He needed your help, so he was really nice to you first, right?"

"Wrong! He wasted 10 minutes of my precious time, *pretending* he cares about me. Then he wants me to take more of my time to do his hot job. And I have this other hot job."

She took a deep breath and then continued. "Do you know I pass by that man in the hall several times a day and he doesn't even acknowledge me-- not a hello, not a smile, not even a nod. But when he wants something, all of a sudden he is my friend."

"Young man, when you need my help and I'm busy, don't butter me up, just ask. Be nice to me when you don't need something from me."

I learned a lesson that day that changed my life: *Shyness is no excuse.*

Before that day, I used to walk down the hall and avoid eye contact with anyone I didn't know well, using my shyness as the excuse.

From that day on I fought my shyness and started walking down the hall with my head up, seeking eye contact. When I made eye contact or got close, I would smile and greet anyone I passed whether I knew them or not.

Repeatedly greeting strangers in the hall helped me gradually chip away at my shyness. It also helped me develop "nodding acquaintances" with fellow employees. They were no longer strangers.

Then, if I had an emergency and needed someone to drop everything and help me, I didn't have to suddenly establish a positive rapport with them; I could be considerate of their time and just get right to the point.

Years later, there was a time when I had to get an emergency package shipped to a customer by the next day. I went to shipping at 1:15 in the afternoon and introduced myself to the clerk, with whom I had a "nodding acquaintance" from walking down the halls.

"Hi. My name's Walt."

"Hi, I'm Sue."

"Sue, can you please help me? This has to go out today. Can we make this happen?"

"Walt, I'm busy … but if you can get a charge number, fill out this form and bring it back to me by 2, we can have it ready for Fed-Ex to pick up at 3."

"Thanks, Sue."

Takeaway

Do not underestimate the power of the simple act of greeting the people you pass in the hall. Good morning, hello, hi, or even a nod or a smile. It will help you overcome shyness and make you more effective.

Chapter 18
Stand Up and Speak Up

The number-one fear is the fear of speaking in public. It's even more common than the fear of dying. However, it is possible to overcome it. Even later in life. And when you overcome your fear of public speaking, it will make it easier to overcome other fears.

Here are some rules to follow:

- Just because you couldn't speak in public before doesn't mean you can't do it now.
- When opportunity knocks, answer the door.
- Invest in yourself.
- You can't just study; you have to do the work.
- There's no elevator to success. You have to take the stairs.
- Use personal stories.
- Don't try to be perfect.
- Make eye contact.
- Record yourself.

- Cross-train

- Breathe.

- Set deadlines.

- Be nice.

I made a decision to overcome my fear of public speaking and take the first step in that direction. Then I took more steps. I am now speaking, performing in improv and sketch-comedy shows, doing stand-up, and hosting a radio show.

You can overcome your fear of public speaking too! What amazing experiences might await you after you do?

The world needs to know you exist. So stand up and speak up!

www.ingramcontent.com/pod-product-compliance
Lightning Source LLC
Chambersburg PA
CBHW052117070526
44584CB00017B/2535